GOD

SO LOVED THE WORLD

He Made

NURSES

SO THAT EVERYONE

Could Be

Loved

AND CARED FOR

NOTEBOOK

This Notebook Belongs To:

Phone:

E-Mail:

www.InspirationalWares.com

HABIT TRACKER

HABIT/DAY	1	2	3	4	5	6	7	8	9	10	11	12	13	14	15	16	17	18	19	20	21	22	23	24	25

For more amazing journals and adult coloring books from Penelope Pewter, visit:

Amazon.com
CreateSpace.com
RWSquaredMedia.Wordpress.com

She Believed She Could
So She Did
Adult Coloring Book with
Inspirational Quotes
A Coloring Book for Grown-Ups Providing Relaxation
and Encouragement for Women

She Believed She Could
So She Did Adult Coloring Book
with Inspirational Quotes

The
BE A PINEAPPLE
STAND TALL,
WEAR A CROWN,
& BE SWEET
ON THE INSIDE
Adult Coloring Book

The Be A Pineapple Adult
Coloring Book

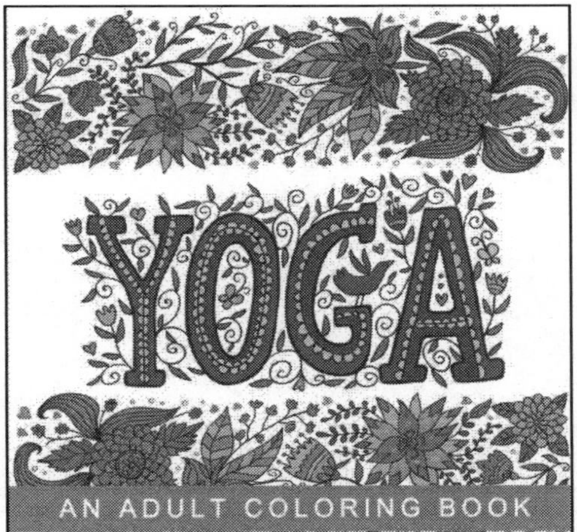
YOGA
AN ADULT COLORING BOOK

YOGA
An Adult Coloring Book

The Adult Coloring
Book for
Coffee Lovers
A Meditation and
Stress Relief Coloring
Book for Grown-Ups

The Adult Coloring Book for
Coffee Lovers

10715046R00062

Made in the USA
Middletown, DE
12 November 2018